The Alphabet of Gregg Shorthand

CONSONANTS

Written forward:

K	G	R	L	N	M	T	D	TH

Written downward:

P	B	F	V	CH	J	S	SH

H	NG	NK

(A dot)

VOWELS

A-group

Short	ă as in	cat	
Medium	ä " "	calm	
Long	ā " "	came	

O-group

Short	ŏ as in	hot	
Medium	aw " "	audit	
Long	ō " "	ode	

E-group

Short	ĭ as in	din	
Medium	ĕ " "	den	
Long	ē " "	dean	

OO-group

Short	ŭ as in	tuck	
Medium	o͝o " "	took	
Long	o͞o " "	doom	

DIPHTHONGS

	Composed of					Composed of		
ū	ē-o͞o	as in	*unit*		oi	aw-ē	as in	*oil*
ow	ä-o͞o	" "	*owl*		ī	ä-ē	" "	*isle*

Made in United States
North Haven, CT
21 June 2024

53892585R00076